11-18

MIAMI
DOLPHINS

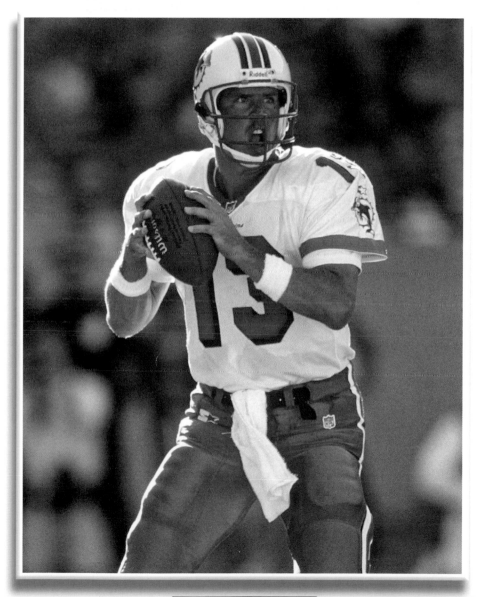

by Dave McMahon

Printed in the United States of America,
North Mankato, Minnesota
062010
092010

 THIS BOOK CONTAINS AT LEAST 10% RECYCLED MATERIALS.

Editor: Chrös McDougall
Copy Editor: Nicholas Cafarelli
Interior Design and Production: Christa Schneider
Cover Design: Christa Schneider

Photo Credits: Wilfredo Lee/AP Images, cover; NFL Photos/AP Images, 1, 4, 6, 9, 11, 12, 14, 20, 25, 34, 36, 42 (top), 42 (bottom), 43 (middle), 47; AP Images, 17, 19, 31, 33, 42 (middle); Steve Starr/AP Images, 23; Doug Jennings/AP Images, 27, 43 (top); Kathy Willens/AP Images, 28; Matt York/AP Images, 39; Hans Deryk/AP Images, 41, 43 (bottom); David Drapkin/AP Images, 44

Library of Congress Cataloging-in-Publication Data
McMahon, Dave.
  Miami Dolphins / Dave McMahon.
      p. cm. — (Inside the NFL)
  Includes index.
  ISBN 978-1-61714-017-4
  1. Miami Dolphins (Football team)—History—Juvenile literature. I. Title.
  GV956.M47M37 2010
  796.332'6409759381—dc22
                          2010015884

TABLE OF CONTENTS

CHAPTER 1

PERFECTION

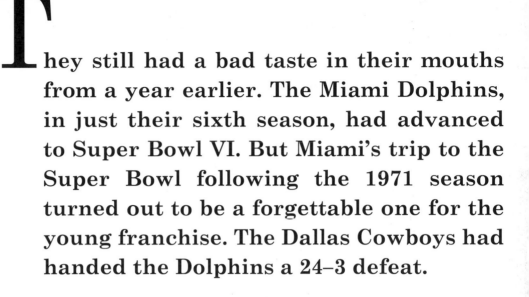

They still had a bad taste in their mouths from a year earlier. The Miami Dolphins, in just their sixth season, had advanced to Super Bowl VI. But Miami's trip to the Super Bowl following the 1971 season turned out to be a forgettable one for the young franchise. The Dallas Cowboys had handed the Dolphins a 24–3 defeat.

The 1972 season, however, was shaping up to be one for the record books. The team ended a perfect season at 14–0. The Dolphins then opened the playoffs with a six-point victory over the Cleveland Browns. In the American Football Conference (AFC) Championship Game, they beat the Pittsburgh Steelers by four points. After 16 games, the Dolphins were still perfect. All they needed now was a victory over the Washington Redskins in Super Bowl VII.

DOLPHINS RUNNING BACK LARRY CSONKA RUSHED FOR 112 YARDS ON 15 CARRIES AGAINST THE WASHINGTON REDSKINS IN SUPER BOWL VII.

MIAMI QUARTERBACK BOB GRIESE LINES UP AGAINST THE WASHINGTON REDSKINS IN SUPER BOWL VII IN LOS ANGELES, CALIFORNIA.

The Dolphins came into the game prepared. Coach Don Shula had joined the team in 1970. He had already lost two Super Bowls before 1972. One had been with Miami and the other with the Baltimore Colts. This time he made sure his team was ready.

SHULA'S DOMINANCE

Coach Don Shula finished his career with the most wins in NFL history with a 33-year record of 328–156–6. Those victories extended beyond his 26 years in Miami. With the Dolphins, Shula went 257–133–2. He also went 71–23–4 with the Baltimore Colts. Shula took six teams to the Super Bowl. He was inducted into the Pro Football Hall of Fame in 1997.

The Dolphins had a consistent offense. In later years, the team would rely on quarterback Bob Griese to throw the ball. But in 1972, the Dolphins relied mostly on their running game. The team had three powerful running backs in Larry Csonka, Jim Kiick, and Mercury Morris. Shula liked his team to keep the ball in their hands as much as possible.

In Super Bowl VII, the Dolphins quickly began beating up on the Redskins. Griese threw a 28-yard touchdown pass to Howard Twilley in the first quarter. Kiick's 1-yard touchdown run in the second quarter extended their lead to 14–0.

Miami held onto that lead through most of the second half. Then, with less than three minutes left, the team had a chance to put the game out of reach. They brought Garo Yepremian

POSSESSION OFFENSE

"Our biggest strength was ball control on offense. We just . . . in many games that year we'd win the toss, get the ball, have an eight- or nine-minute drive, score a touchdown, go ahead 7–0, our defense would hold them, their offense would be three-and-out, and we'd get the ball and repeat. When the first quarter was over we were ahead 14–0 and the other team had the ball for three or six plays. Our time of possessions was just a real trademark of that football team."

—Don Shula on the 1972 offense

out to kick a field goal. The Pro Football Hall of Fame later named the kicker to their 1970s All-Decade team. But he would not make this kick.

Bill Brundige blocked the attempt. Yepremian picked it up. He attempted to throw a pass, but the ball slipped out of his hand and went straight up in the air. He got a hand on it again, but Redskins cornerback Mike Bass pulled it in. Bass took the fumble return 49 yards for a touchdown. The Dolphins' lead had been cut to 14–7.

"It was a bizarre play, it's hard to believe it could ever happen in a professional football game," Shula said. "It was just such a shock, and I think all of us on the sidelines, when it happened, realized the magnitude of the play, and that the Redskins, who hadn't done anything the whole ball game, were back with a chance to tie."

The Dolphins got the ball back, but had to punt after failing to get a first down. Washington took over with a little more than a minute left—and the chance to tie the game with a touchdown.

Now it was up to Miami to hold on. The Dolphins were known for their "No-Name Defense" during the early 1970s.

DON'T MISS IT

"We lose this game, I'm going to kill you!"

—Dolphins linebacker Nick Buoniconti on the sideline to Garo Yepremian in Super Bowl VII. Buoniconti made the quip after the kicker threw a botched field-goal attempt into the hands of Washington's Mike Bass.

The defense did not have as many stars as the offense. Still, it had helped Miami win four AFC East division championships. With time running out in Super Bowl VII, the "No-Name Defense" held on again. Jake Scott had two interceptions in the game. He would later become the first defensive back to be the Most Valuable Player (MVP) of a Super Bowl.

The Dolphins of 1972 became the first and only National Football League (NFL) team to finish a season undefeated and then

MIAMI DOLPHINS KICKER GARO YEPREMIAN CHASES THE BALL AFTER HIS FIELD GOAL ATTEMPT WAS BLOCKED IN SUPER BOWL VII.

KEEP IT SIMPLE

The Dolphins did not allow their scoring opportunities to slip away during their run to perfection in 1972. Quarterback Bob Griese would find wide receiver Paul Warfield with a short pass. Or, fullback Larry Csonka would pound his way into the end zone in short yardage plays. The Dolphins did not pretend to be flashy. In fact, some people called them "boring."

"When I reflect back, that was a very businesslike team," coach Don Shula said. "It was a very intelligent football team, and we were sometimes characterized as a team that was not an exciting team because of the way that we dominated games. We took pride in that approach. It was a very professional approach, and it was a very thorough approach as to how to win a football game."

The Dolphins' offense was very effective, though. They led the NFL in points and yards during that 1972 season.

win the Super Bowl. Some people called it the perfect season.

"It seemed like I had been so focused and I can say the same for my teammates, so focused on getting back to [the Super Bowl] to show the critics who said that we're just another team. . . ." Dolphins future Hall of Fame wide receiver Paul Warfield said. "I don't believe that the 17–0 [record] registered on anybody. The press was aware of it, but it was not as big a deal as it is today, simply because teams are . . . [now] trying to reach and surpass [it]," Warfield added.

Long after the Dolphins' 1972 perfect season, other teams are still trying to reach and surpass that record.

MERCURY MORRIS RUNS PAST A REDSKINS PLAYER ON A KICKOFF RETURN IN SUPER BOWL VII.

CHAPTER 2

MAKING THE DOLPHINS

Joseph Robbie once ran for governor in his native South Dakota. That campaign failed. But Robbie proved to be a winner to everyone in Miami who loved football. Robbie graduated from Sisseton High School in 1935. He earned a degree from Northern State College. Then he went on to acquire his law degree from the University of South Dakota. There, Robbie made a friend who proved to be important later in his life.

MR. STADIUM

Joe Robbie helped fund the construction of Joe Robbie Stadium in Miami. He also served as the national fund-raising chairman for the construction of the DakotaDome in Vermillion, South Dakota. The Dome is now home to the University of South Dakota football, basketball, volleyball, swimming, diving, and track-and-field teams.

Robbie moved east to Minneapolis, Minnesota, in 1953. There, he used his talents as an urban planner, someone who helps guide development in a city. He also got involved in football, thanks to his friend from the University of South Dakota.

BOB GRIESE, SHOWN IN 1974, HELPED THE DOLPHINS BREAK FREE OF THEIR LOSING WAYS. HE PLAYED 14 SEASONS FOR MIAMI.

JOE ROBBIE, SHOWN IN 1970, BROUGHT PROFESSIONAL FOOTBALL TO MIAMI WHEN HE BOUGHT THE EXPANSION DOLPHINS IN 1965.

That friend, Joe Foss, was the commissioner of the American Football League (AFL). In 1965, Robbie traveled to Washington DC to meet with Foss. While there, Foss encouraged Robbie to apply for the AFL's expansion team in Miami.

THOMAS ALSO HELPED

Danny Thomas joined Joe Robbie as a founder of the Dolphins. He was also the founder in 1962 of the St. Jude's Children's Research Hospital in Memphis, Tennessee. Both Thomas's and Robbie's parents were of Lebanese descent. Thomas was a famous television actor and comedian.

Robbie went to Miami in May of that year to meet with Mayor Robert King High. The two talked about whether a new pro team could play in the Orange Bowl stadium. On May 6, 1965, the mayor agreed to invite the AFL to Miami. The AFL agreed to expand for the 1966 season. On August 16, 1965, Joe Robbie and television star Danny Thomas were awarded the Miami expansion team. The price was $7.5 million.

Robbie and Thomas started to build their team in the AFL's college draft. Miami selected University of Kentucky quarterback Rick Norton and Illinois running back Jim Grabowski in the first round. Those players proved to be unremarkable. Norton went 1–10 as a starter in his four years in Miami. Grabowski opted to play for the Green Bay Packers of the NFL.

NAME THAT TEAM

A fan contest drew 19,843 entries to name the AFL expansion team in Miami. A total of 622 contestants suggested "Dolphins." Team owner Joe Robbie said he liked the name because "the dolphin is one of the fastest and smartest creatures in the sea."

The expansion draft took place in January 1966. That also allowed the Dolphins to select 31 players from the eight existing AFL teams. One of those selected was offensive tackle Norm Evans from Houston. He ended up playing 10 seasons with the Dolphins.

Less than three weeks after the AFL expansion draft, George Wilson became the first head coach of the Dolphins. He had been coach of the Detroit Lions before joining Miami. Wilson posted a record of 53–45–6 with the Lions and had won the NFL championship in 1957. His four seasons in Miami were not nearly

THE AFL

The AFL was created in 1959 as a rival league to the NFL. When it began play in 1960, few people expected the league to survive. But the league did just that. In fact, by 1966, the AFL and NFL agreed to merge into one league. When the merger was complete in 1970, the AFL and three NFL teams became today's American Football Conference. The remainder of the NFL teams became today's National Football Conference. Each conference's winner now plays in the Super Bowl.

The AFL began with eight teams, all of which are in today's NFL. They were the Boston Patriots (New England), Buffalo Bills, Dallas Texans (Kansas City Chiefs), Denver Broncos, Houston Oilers (Tennessee Titans), Los Angeles Chargers (San Diego), New York Titans (Jets), and the Oakland Raiders. The Miami Dolphins joined the AFL in 1966 and the Cincinnati Bengals became the league's tenth team in 1968.

as successful. Wilson compiled a record of 15–39–2 before giving way to Don Shula.

The Dolphins' first season in 1966 ended with a record of 3–11. The 1967 season brought more of the same. However, Miami's 4–10 record did include a star in the making. In September, quarterback John Stofa broke his right ankle. Rookie Bob Griese replaced him. Griese threw a 68-yard touchdown pass during the Dolphins' 35–21 win over the Denver Broncos at the Orange Bowl. In November, Griese's fourth-quarter heroics showed up again. This time it was against Buffalo. With 1:01 left, Griese threw a 31-yard touchdown pass to Howard Twilley. That was the game-winning pass as Miami won 17–14.

It did not take Griese long to make an impact, even with

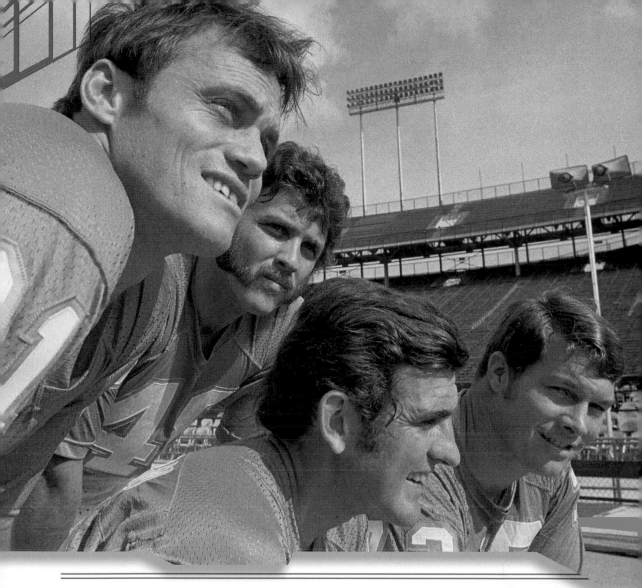

FOUR MEMBERS OF THE ORIGINAL MIAMI DOLPHINS, *FROM LEFT,* HOWARD TWILLEY, BOB PETRELLA, KARL NOONAN, AND NORM EVANS

an average club. During his second year as a pro, Griese threw for 2,473 yards. He also threw 21 touchdowns to 16 interceptions. The yardage was a career high.

He only beat the touchdown mark when he threw 22 in 1977.

Griese offered a bright start. But four years of poor play were more than enough for the team's fans. Miami's 15–39–2 record in that time span was dismal. Wilson had won four NFL championships as a player with the Chicago Bears. But he was relieved of his coaching duties following the 1969 season.

One newspaper columnist had an idea for how to stop the losing in Miami. "Why don't you go right to the top and get the best there is? Don Shula."

The Dolphins began their search for a new coach after the 1969 season. When Robbie called Shula to discuss an offer, Shula's response was, "I can't talk now." Shula then hung up the phone. He was the coach of the Baltimore Colts at the time. When Robbie called, a fight between two Colts assistant coaches was breaking out on Shula's front lawn. He had to stop it.

But Shula did talk with Robbie again soon. He agreed to take over as coach of the Miami Dolphins. Shula's arrival in 1970 brought with it a newfound commitment to success. For Griese, Shula also provided a springboard to his career. That boost eventually helped Griese land in the Pro Football Hall of Fame.

DON SHULA WAS BROUGHT IN TO CHANGE THE FORTUNES OF THE DOLPHINS. HE HAD GUIDED BALTIMORE TO SEVEN STRAIGHT WINNING SEASONS.

CHAPTER 3

PRESERVING PERFECTION

Don Shula took over as the Dolphins' coach in 1970. In the season before, the Dolphins had been a lowly 3–10–1. Shula's first step to success was creating a practice plan. It was a drastic change for the players.

There were four practices a day. The 7:00 a.m. start included special teams and the kicking game. A 7:45 a.m. breakfast was followed by a 9:30 a.m. meeting to cover the details of that day's upcoming sessions. At 10:00 a.m., the running game (both offense and defense) took priority. Lunch was at 11:30 a.m.; then came another meeting at 3:00 p.m. One half hour later, the passing game (both offense and defense) took center stage. Dinner at 6:00 p.m. was followed by a 7:30 p.m. practice that was used to work on corrections. This practice lasted until dark. After a 9:30 p.m. meeting, the team was dismissed at 10:30 p.m.

LARRY CSONKA CARRIES THE BALL DURING A 1971 GAME AGAINST THE LOS ANGELES RAMS. THE DOLPHINS WON THE GAME 20–14.

"My players couldn't believe what I was asking them to do," Shula said. "There was a lot of moaning and groaning from the guys. 'Four practices a day!' 'This is unheard of.' 'What's he trying to do? Kill us?'"

Shula was merely preparing the team for the most successful start to a coaching career in NFL history. The Dolphins reached Super Bowl VI after the 1971 season, but lost to the Dallas Cowboys. They entered the 1972 season with hopes of taking that next step.

Midway through the perfect 1972 season, however, Miami fans began to worry. In Week 5, Bob Griese broke his leg. Earl Morrall replaced him as quarterback.

Under Shula's guidance, Morrall picked up right where Griese left off. Griese returned later in the season and started Super Bowl VII. The early 1970s, however, were a running era for the Dolphins.

The Miami offense had a three-headed monster in the backfield. In 1972 running backs Mercury Morris and Larry Csonka became the first duo in NFL history to rush for at least 1,000 yards in a season. Star running back Jim Kiick joined them. The three led the Dolphins to the Super Bowl for three straight seasons, including Super Bowl VIII after the 1973 season.

EARL MORRALL FILLED IN JUST FINE FOR BOB GRIESE AT QUARTERBACK DURING THE DOLPHINS' PERFECT 1972 SEASON.

NOT MUCH TIME

" Sure, he's got all summer."

—Dolphins owner Joe Robbie, when asked in 1970 whether he would give new coach Don Shula enough time to produce a winning team

In the team's history, the Dolphins have had four games in which two players each rushed for at least 100 yards. Csonka and Kiick accomplished the feat twice, both times in 1971.

Morris joined Don Nottingham in achieving the 100-yard benchmark in 1975. Morris also excelled as kick returner. In the 1971 season, Morris led the AFC with a 28.2-yard average on kickoff returns.

Together, the three running backs put up numbers that might never be matched on the same team ever again. Csonka is the team's all-time leading rusher with 6,737 career yards. As of the end of the 2009 season, Ricky Williams was next. Ronnie Brown was third, and Morris was fourth. Kiick sat fifth all-time. However, beginning in 1978, the NFL regular season expanded from 14 to 16 games.

The Dolphins returned to the Super Bowl after the 1973 season. They easily defeated the Minnesota Vikings 24–7 in Super Bowl VIII. Csonka was named MVP of the game. He ran for 145 yards and two touchdowns on 33 attempts. Csonka also landed in the Pro Football Hall of Fame after a spectacular career.

"When I was playing and practicing in that heat in July and August in Miami with shoulder pads on, it just vaporized me," said Csonka, who later moved to Alaska. "Shula would always come over and look at me and say, 'Where are you? I know you're not here. You're just on

BOB GRIESE (12) HANDS OFF TO RUNNING BACK JIM KIICK (21) DURING A 1971 GAME AGAINST THE LOS ANGELES RAMS.

automatic pilot.' I was up here [in Alaska] in my mind, fishing in a stream."

Meanwhile, the Dolphins' "No-Name Defense" was a fitting nickname for the Super Bowl-bound teams of the 1970s.

Linebacker Nick Buoniconti, undersized at 5-feet-11 and 220 pounds, led the group. He ended up in the Pro Football Hall of Fame. He is the only player from the Dolphins' defense to achieve such glory.

BUONICONTI A GEM

Linebacker Nick Buoniconti starred at the University of Notre Dame before becoming an NFL legend. Buoniconti has also been a beacon of hope for many people who suffer from spinal cord injuries. In 1985, his son Marc suffered a devastating spinal cord injury. Since then, Nick has spent much time raising awareness and funds for spinal cord injury research. He helped found The Miami Project to Cure Paralysis. Through his involvement, more than $150 million has been raised to support its research programs. The Project has become known as the world's leading center for spinal cord injuries.

On the field, Buoniconti was a star linebacker. He played 14 seasons, including seven with Miami. He was an eight-time All-AFL/AFC selection. Buoniconti was inducted into the Pro Football Hall of Fame in 2001.

Since the perfect 1972 season, the Dolphins players from that team have celebrated when every NFL team has at least one loss. The players on the 1985 Dolphins were also able to use that legacy as motivation.

Behind a strong defense, the 1985 Chicago Bears looked poised to join the 1972 Dolphins in having a perfect season. The Bears were nearly unstoppable. Defensive coordinator Buddy Ryan had introduced the "46 Defense." Behind that scheme, the Bears had limited the opposing team to an average of 12.4 points per game.

Then, in Week 13 of the 16-week season, the Bears ran into the Miami Dolphins. The Dolphins were a good team. They had reached the Super Bowl after the 1982 and 1984 seasons. But they also had a

RECEIVER NAT MOORE AND THE DOLPHINS ENDED CHICAGO'S PUSH FOR A
PERFECT SEASON IN 1985 WITH A 38–24 WIN.

special motivation to beat the Bears. On *Monday Night Football*, the Dolphins handed the Bears their lone loss of the season, 38–24.

"The Bears in '85, first of all, were a great football team, and if we hadn't upset them in that Monday-night game, they could have conceivably been an undefeated team—they were that good," Shula said. "But we dominated that night, and, again, that makes that accomplishment more important in my reflections of my coaching career."

CHAPTER 4

BEST GAME EVER?

The Dolphins' rich history under coach Don Shula included many great players. Eight of them went on to be inducted into the Pro Football Hall of Fame. But great teams often have more than a few star players. The other players also have an important role in the team's success.

Just ask Don Strock. He was one half of the quarterback duo known as "WoodStrock." The name came about because Strock and the other quarterback, David Woodley, often rotated in and out of the starting role. Strock was not a superstar, but he was ready when called upon.

In January 1982, Miami hosted the San Diego Chargers

WHO'S BEHIND CENTER?

In 1980, future Hall of Famer Bob Griese started the season at quarterback. He was replaced by backup Don Strock in a Week 1 loss. Then Strock relieved Griese for a win; Griese replaced Strock for a win; Griese stepped in for David Woodley; and Woodley took over for Griese in Week 5.

MIAMI'S BACKUP QUARTERBACK DON STROCK THROWS A PASS IN A 1979 GAME AGAINST THE NEW YORK JETS.

in a playoff game at the Orange Bowl. Woodley, 23, became the youngest quarterback to start a playoff game. But he would not play long. After the first quarter, Miami was down 24–0. Strock took over as quarterback early in the second quarter.

Strock did his best to match Chargers star quarterback Dan Fouts. One of Strock's plays became among the most memorable in team history. With six seconds left in the first half, Strock threw a 15-yard pass to wide receiver Duriel Harris. After catching it, Harris pitched the ball back to running back Tony Nathan. Nathan then ran the ball 25 yards for the touchdown. The "hook and lateral" play cut the Chargers' lead to 24–17 in less than one quarter.

"I've never seen anything like it," Strock recalled. He was referring to the fans' celebration, which lasted well into halftime. "It was like we were still on the field. It was that loud. We were in the locker room, what—10, 15 minutes?—and it never stopped!"

Strock only got better as the game went on. In fact, Strock put up the best numbers of his career. He went 29 of 43 passing for 403 yards and four touchdowns.

Fouts played well, too. It was the first game in NFL history in which both quarterbacks threw for more than 400 yards. The teams were tied after regulation. In overtime, both teams

SEE YOU LATER

What caused the demise of the Dolphins after winning two Super Bowls in the early 1970s? It was due in large part to the formation of the World Football League (WFL). The WFL was a short-lived pro football league during the mid-1970s. Larry Csonka, Jim Kiick, and Paul Warfield all left the team following the 1974 season to play in the WFL.

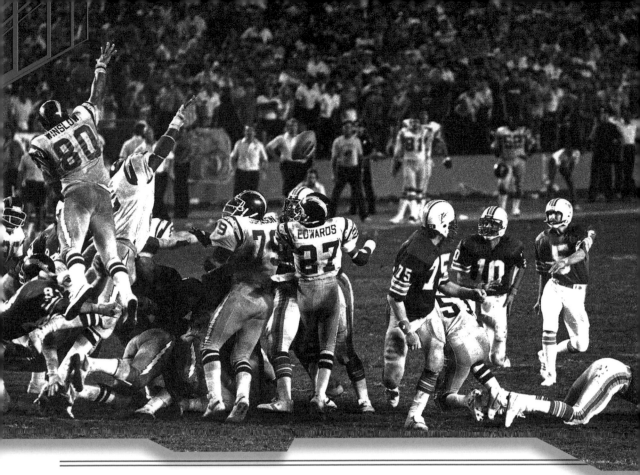

THE CHARGERS BLOCK THE DOLPHINS' OVERTIME FIELD GOAL ATTEMPT BEFORE MAKING THEIR OWN IN A 1982 PLAYOFF GAME.

missed a field goal. Then San Diego's Rolf Benirschke booted a 29-yard field goal with 1:08 left in overtime for the win. San Diego's 41–38 win was the highest scoring game in playoff history.

Fouts set NFL playoff records for most completions (33), most attempts (53), and most yards (433). Chargers tight end Kellen Winslow was battling dehydration and cramps by the end of the game. But he still set a playoff record for most receptions (13 for 166 yards).

The Dolphins rebounded. They returned to the Super Bowl after the 1982 season. However, they ended up losing 27–17 to the Washington Redskins.

The 1983 draft signaled a new era for Miami. With their first-round pick, the team selected Dan Marino, a quarterback from the University of Pittsburgh. Marino would go on to be considered one of the greatest quarterbacks in NFL history. But in the 1983 draft, some teams thought he was a risk. In fact, 26 teams passed on him. Miami selected him with the twenty-seventh pick.

BOB GRIESE

After 14 seasons with the Dolphins, Bob Griese retired after the 1980 season. During his career, he played in eight Pro Bowls or AFL All-Star Games. Griese also became the fourteenth passer in football history to throw for more than 25,000 yards in a career. He was inducted into the Pro Football Hall of Fame in 1990. Griese went on to become a sports broadcaster.

"I'd been hoping Marino would be there, but I didn't see any logical way he could," Shula said. "I'd seen him in the Hula Bowl and Senior Bowl. All he'd done was win the MVP in both."

Marino replaced Woodley after five games in 1983. He went on to be named NFL Rookie of the Year. He also became the first rookie quarterback to start in the Pro Bowl. One year later, Marino had the Dolphins back in the Super Bowl.

"I'm throwing the way I've always thrown," Marino said after taking over as starting quarterback in 1983. "I'm reading coverages better because it's a full-time job now, an all-day thing instead of just a few hours in the afternoon. Plus I've got Coach Shula working with me."

ROOKIE QUARTERBACK DAN MARINO LOOKS FOR A RECEIVER DURING A 1983 PLAYOFF GAME AGAINST THE SEATTLE SEAHAWKS. SEATTLE WON 27–20.

CHAPTER 5

MAN ON A MISSION

Dan Marino had a record-breaking season in 1984. He set season records with 48 touchdown passes, 362 completions, and 5,084 passing yards. The previous touchdown record had been only 36 in a season. Marino also became the first quarterback to throw for 5,000 yards in a season.

Marino again looked invincible in the AFC Championship Game after that season. He led the Dolphins 45–28 past the Pittsburgh Steelers. Fans were eager to see what he would do at Super Bowl XIX.

"If he's just a little off, just once or twice, maybe we can get an interception," said Tony Dungy, the Steelers' defensive coordinator. "But he was not off. It was his day."

> ### THEY SAID IT
>
> "You were basically at Dan's [Marino] mercy. All the great ones see the game so quickly that when everybody else is running around like a chicken with his head cut off, they know exactly where they want to go with the ball. It's like they see everything in slow motion."
> —Hall of Fame defensive back Ronnie Lott

MIAMI'S HALL OF FAME CENTER DWIGHT STEPHENSON GETS READY FOR A PLAY IN 1984. HE PLAYED EIGHT SEASONS WITH THE DOLPHINS.

Marino had reached his first Super Bowl in 1984 after only his second season. He threw 50 passes there but connected for only one touchdown. It was an otherwise forgettable game for Dolphins fans. Miami lost 38–16 to star quarterback Joe Montana and the San Francisco 49ers. After Marino's successful year, Dolphins fans thought it was only a matter of time before they returned to the Super Bowl.

"You don't break all the records Dan Marino has broken this season without doing something right," Shula said after the AFC Championship Game. "Teams have tried all kinds of schemes against him—drop eight men and rush only

DAN MARINO TAKES A SNAP DURING A 1994 GAME AGAINST THE BUFFALO BILLS. MARINO SET MANY PASSING RECORDS DURING HIS CAREER.

TALENT SCOUT

Dan Marino was one of the most feared players in the NFL. "He's a phenom," Buffalo defensive end Bruce Smith told *Sports Illustrated* in 1996. "There couldn't have been a better passer ever. I mean, the guy just doesn't miss. And he's not fast, but you can't catch him. Playing him twice a year is like playing [New York Yankees great Joe] DiMaggio all the time."

Even Marino said that he sometimes felt unstoppable. "There were times on the field when I felt like I couldn't miss," Marino said. "The ball was always on time, it was always catchable, and I was making the right decisions on who to throw to."

The teams that passed on drafting Marino were kicking themselves later. The quarterback was selected to nine Pro Bowls during his career and left Miami with dozens of offensive records. He was enshrined in the Pro Football Hall of Fame in 2005.

three, or blitz everybody, or combinations. Pittsburgh tried the combinations today. Dan had the answers."

Marino never made it back to a second Super Bowl. But he continued to set new records for a quarterback. One that Marino was particularly proud of was his consecutive-games-started by a quarterback streak. He played in 145 games straight until a leg injury set him back in the fifth game of the 1993 season.

"The consecutive-game thing, I'm really proud of that," Marino said. "Lining up and playing every week—your teammates knowing you're going to be there. The rest of the records come from playing every week."

Marino created many memorable plays with his accurate passing. One became known as the "Clock Play." In a 1994 game, the Dolphins trailed the New York Jets by 18 points on the road. Marino led the Dolphins on a 21-point surge in the second half. With about 30 seconds left, Miami had the ball on the Jets' 8-yard line. The Dolphins were trailing 24–21. Since they were out of timeouts, most people expected Marino to spike the ball and stop the clock. That would give the Dolphins time to send out the kicking team to try for a field goal.

Marino signaled that he was going to spike the ball to

STILL PERFECT

Miami's perfect season with a Super Bowl title in 1972 continues to set the standard in the NFL. Teams have had their sights set on matching the record, but none have been able to do so. The New England Patriots went 16–0 in the regular season in 2007 but lost in Super Bowl XLII. The 2009 Indianapolis Colts started their season 14–0 before losing their last two regular-season games.

FORMER DOLPHINS RUNNING BACK MERCURY MORRIS TALKS ABOUT MIAMI'S 1972 PERFECT SEASON AT A NEWS CONFERENCE IN 2008.

stop the clock. But it was a decoy. Instead, Marino took the snap and dropped back to find an open receiver. With only 22 seconds remaining, he found wide receiver Mark Ingram in the end zone. It was Ingram's fourth touchdown of the game. The Dolphins won 28–24.

"Use it now!" backup quarterback Bernie Kosar said to Marino through the helmet radio. "Go for the rookie [defending Ingram]!"

Shula retired after the 1995 season. New coach Jimmy Johnson helped guide Miami to the playoffs in three of the next four seasons. But after the 1999 season, Marino was 38 years old. He decided to retire.

By this time, Marino owned 19 NFL records and shared five others. After the 2009 season, his 61,361 passing yards, 420 passing touchdowns, and 4,967 completions all ranked second all-time in the NFL, behind Brett Favre.

Miami has had successful seasons since Marino retired.

However, the team has not been able to turn them into a Super Bowl appearance. Dave Wannstedt took over as coach in 2000. He directed the team to 11–5 records and playoff berths in each of his first two seasons. His replacement in 2005, Nick Saban, was not as successful. He returned to college football after two years with the Dolphins.

Cam Cameron's one year as head coach in 2007 produced a 1–15 record. The 2007 Dolphins lost their first 13 games before they defeated Baltimore 22–16. Things began to turn around in December 2007. Dolphins owner Wayne Huizenga hired Bill Parcells as the team's executive vice president of football operations. Parcells had won two Super Bowls as a head coach. His first move was to hire former Dallas Cowboys assistant head coach Tony Sparano.

CLOSE CALL

In 2007, the Dolphins were on the verge of becoming the first team in NFL history to go without a victory in a 16-game regular season. A 22–16 win over Baltimore ended that possibility. The Detroit Lions took "worst team in history" honors in 2008 when they went 0–16. Tampa Bay went 0–14 in 1976, its first season in the league.

DOLPHINS RUNNING BACK RICKY WILLIAMS PREPARES TO BLOCK FOR QUARTERBACK CHAD HENNE IN A 2009 GAME AGAINST HOUSTON.

The Dolphins went 11–5 and made the playoffs in 2008. That was in large part due to their effective use of the wild-cat formation, in which the ball is snapped to the running back. But one year later, they struggled again, finishing 7–9.

The recent Miami Dolphins teams have been far from perfect, but their fans can take pride in knowing that their team is still the only one to complete the perfect season.

NO STABILITY

During his 26 years in Miami, coach Don Shula guided the Dolphins to the playoffs 16 times. In the eight seasons leading into 2010, the Dolphins have made one trip to the playoffs under the guidance of four different head coaches.

TIMELINE

1965	Minneapolis lawyer Joseph Robbie meets AFL commissioner Joe Foss in Washington DC on March 3. Foss advises Robbie to apply for an expansion franchise in Miami.
1965	On August 16, the AFL awards its first expansion franchise to Joseph Robbie and television star Danny Thomas for $7.5 million.
1966	The Dolphins defeat Denver 24–7 on October 16 for the first win in franchise history. That ends a string of nine losses, including four in the preseason.
1970	After seven years as coach of the Baltimore Colts, Don Shula becomes head coach and vice president of the Dolphins on February 18.
1972	The Dallas Cowboys defeat Miami 24–3 in Super Bowl VI on January 16 in New Orleans, Louisiana.
1972	The Dolphins go 14–0 in the regular season. On January 14, 1973, the Dolphins cap a perfect 17–0 season by winning Super Bowl VII 14–7 over Washington.
1974	The Dolphins win their second Super Bowl championship in a row with a 24–7 victory over the Minnesota Vikings on January 13. Larry Csonka gains 145 yards rushing on his way to being named MVP.
1981	Bob Griese retires on June 25 after a 14-year career with the Dolphins. The six-time Pro Bowl selection guided the Dolphins to Super Bowl victories after the 1972 and 1973 seasons.

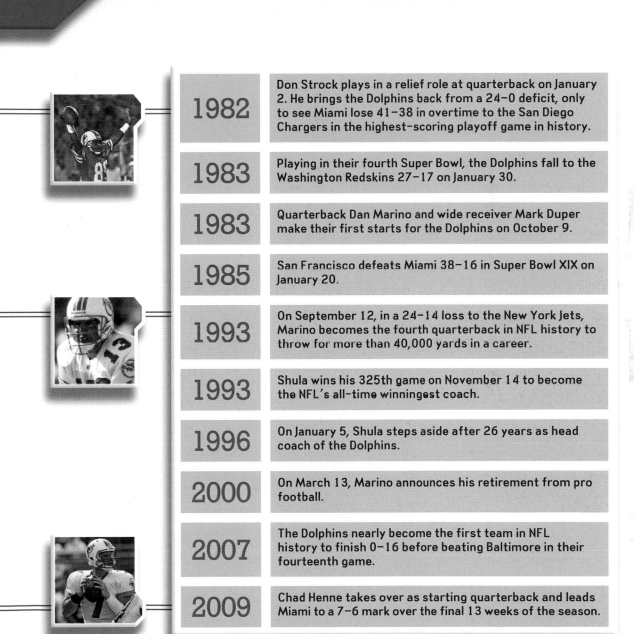

1982	Don Strock plays in a relief role at quarterback on January 2. He brings the Dolphins back from a 24–0 deficit, only to see Miami lose 41–38 in overtime to the San Diego Chargers in the highest-scoring playoff game in history.
1983	Playing in their fourth Super Bowl, the Dolphins fall to the Washington Redskins 27–17 on January 30.
1983	Quarterback Dan Marino and wide receiver Mark Duper make their first starts for the Dolphins on October 9.
1985	San Francisco defeats Miami 38–16 in Super Bowl XIX on January 20.
1993	On September 12, in a 24–14 loss to the New York Jets, Marino becomes the fourth quarterback in NFL history to throw for more than 40,000 yards in a career.
1993	Shula wins his 325th game on November 14 to become the NFL's all-time winningest coach.
1996	On January 5, Shula steps aside after 26 years as head coach of the Dolphins.
2000	On March 13, Marino announces his retirement from pro football.
2007	The Dolphins nearly become the first team in NFL history to finish 0–16 before beating Baltimore in their fourteenth game.
2009	Chad Henne takes over as starting quarterback and leads Miami to a 7–6 mark over the final 13 weeks of the season.

QUICK STATS

FRANCHISE HISTORY

1966–

SUPER BOWLS
(wins in bold)

1971 (VI), **1972 (VII)**, **1973 (VIII)**, 1982 (XVII), 1984 (XIX)

AFC CHAMPIONSHIP GAMES
(since 1970 AFL-NFL merger)

1971, 1972, 1973, 1982, 1984, 1985, 1992

DIVISION CHAMPIONSHIPS
(since 1970 AFL-NFL merger)

1971, 1972, 1973, 1974, 1979, 1981, 1983, 1984, 1985, 1992, 1994, 2000, 2008

KEY PLAYERS
(position, seasons with team)

Nick Buoniconti (LB, 1969–76)
Mark Clayton (WR, 1983–92)
Larry Csonka (FB, 1968–74, 1979)
Bob Griese (QB, 1967–80)
Bob Kuechenberg (G, 1970–83)
Jim Langer (C, 1970–79)
Larry Little (G, 1969–80)
Dan Marino (QB, 1983–99)
Mercury Morris (RB, 1969–75)
Dwight Stephenson (C, 1980–87)

KEY COACHES

Jimmy Johnson (1996–99): 36–28; 2–3 (playoffs)
Don Shula (1970–95): 257–133–2; 17–14 (playoffs)

HOME FIELDS

Sun Life Stadium (1987–)
   Also known as Joe Robbie
   Stadium, Pro Player Park,
   Pro Player Stadium, Dolphins
   Stadium, Dolphin Stadium, and
   Land Shark Stadium.
Orange Bowl (1966–86)

* All statistics through 2009 season

QUOTES AND ANECDOTES

"The thing that stands out about the Super Bowl was that we were 16–0, going to the Super Bowl against the Washington Redskins, the only team that has ever gotten that far. We were underdogs—16–0, and we were underdogs in the Super Bowl. That just told us that we'd won all these games, but we weren't getting any respect from somebody."
—Bob Griese on Super Bowl XII, which capped Miami's perfect 1972 season

In 1977, Bob Griese became the first player to wear glasses in an NFL game.

Garo Yepremian kicked a field goal to give the Dolphins a victory over the Kansas City Chiefs on December 25, 1971. But by the time he took the field, fans were starting to wonder if the game would ever end. The teams used 82 minutes and 40 seconds of game time—the longest game in NFL history—to decide the outcome. Yepremian scored a decade-high 905 points in the 1970s.

In 1996, there were 18 quarterbacks in the Pro Football Hall of Fame. In Dan Marino's first 10 seasons in the league, he threw for at least 12,000 more yards than any of those 18 had in their first 10 seasons.

Sports Illustrated ranked the 1970–74 Dolphins sixth on its list of the NFL's Greatest Teams.

"It was always banging into things, knocking things over, and he was the kind of dog [that] if he ran away I knew he would come back."
—Don Shula, on why he named his collie puppy "Zonk," Larry Csonka's nickname

45

GLOSSARY

botched

Spoiled because of poor work.

dehydration

Abnormal loss of water from the body due to physical exertion.

draft

A system used by professional sports leagues to select new players in order to spread incoming talent among all teams.

expansion

In sports, to add a franchise or franchises to a league.

hall of fame

A place built to honor noteworthy achievements by athletes in their respective sports.

interleague

Refers to something done by teams in different leagues.

legacy

Anything handed down from the past.

legend

A person who achieves fame.

paralysis

The inability to move a body part.

rookie

A first-year professional athlete.

spike

The act of throwing the ball to the ground to stop the clock.

trademark

A distinctive characteristic by which a person or thing becomes known.

verge

The extreme edge or margin; on the brink of achieving a goal.

FOR MORE INFORMATION

Further Reading

MacCambridge, Michael. *America's Game: The Epic Story of How Pro Football Captured a Nation*. New York, NY: Random House, 2004.

McCollough, Bob. *My Greatest Day in Football*. New York, NY: St. Martin's Press, 2001.

Sports Illustrated. *The Football Book Expanded Edition*. New York, NY: Sports Illustrated Books, 2009.

Web Links

To learn more about the Miami Dolphins, visit ABDO Publishing Company online at **www.abdopublishing.com**. Web sites about the Dolphins are featured on our Book Links page. These links are routinely monitored and updated to provide the most current information available.

Places to Visit

Nova Southeastern University
7500 S.W. 30th St.
Davie, FL 33314
954-452-7004
www.nova.edu
The Dolphins' training and practice facility can accommodate 2,000 fans. In addition to two outdoor football fields, an indoor field opened in 2006.

Pro Football Hall of Fame
2121 George Halas Dr., NW
Canton, OH 44708
330-456-8207
www.profootballhof.com
This hall of fame and museum highlights the greatest players and moments in the history of the National Football League. Ten people affiliated with the Dolphins are enshrined, including Larry Csonka, Dan Marino, and Don Shula.

Sun Life Stadium
2269 Dan Marino Boulevard
Miami Gardens, FL 33056
305-623-6100
www.sunlifestadium.com
The home of the Dolphins since 1987. One of the video boards is the largest in pro sports. The stadium's Gallery of Legends provides a visual tour of Dolphins history.

INDEX

About the Author

Dave McMahon grew up in Newnan, Georgia, and became an instant fan of the Dolphins after watching Don Strock's heroic effort in the 41–38 overtime loss to San Diego during the 1981 season playoffs. A graduate of the University of Notre Dame, Dave has written for a variety of newspapers, magazines, and sports Web sites throughout his career. He is the author of several books for young readers. He lives in Eagan, Minnesota, with his family.